AS JESUS GREW

By Sister Shigeko Yano

English Text by Valerie Bannert

Edited by Mildred Schell

Judson Press

© Shiko-Sha 1972
Original edition published in Japan by
Shiko-Sha Co. Ltd., Tokyo, Japan, 1972

First published in U.S.A. in 1973 by Judson Press, Valley Forge, Pa. 19481

Library of Congress Cataloging in Publication Data

Yano, Shigeko.
    As Jesus grew.

    SUMMARY: A translation of a Japanese narrative poem about the childhood of Jesus.
    Translation of Chiisana Iezusu Sama.
    Poems.
    [1. Jesus Christ—Poetry 2. Japanese poetry—Translations into English. 3. English poetry—Translations from Japanese] I. Title.
PZ8.3.Y35As   895.6'1'5   72-12939
ISBN 0-8170-0592-7

Printed in Japan by Shiko-Sha Co. Ltd., Tokyo

Nazareth!
Such a quiet little town!
Birds fly from clear blue skies
to rest in the branches of trees
and fill the air with their songs.

Nazareth!
Such a peaceful little town!
Here lives the Child of Peace—
Jesus of Nazareth.
Here lives the holy family of love—
Jesus and Mary and Joseph.

"How good the bread smells," thought Jesus,
    watching his mother baking.
"How hungry I am!"

Mary took a small loaf from the outdoor oven—round, brown, and crusty.
She smiled as she held it out to her son.

"A special loaf, just for me," shouted Jesus. "Thank you, Mother."
"Careful, Jesus, don't burn your fingers!" laughed Mary.

Joseph worked with care. He was a fine carpenter.
Jesus watched his every move.

"When I grow up, will I be a carpenter, too?" he asked.

Joseph stopped to look kindly at the boy.
"Jesus," he answered, "when you grow up, you will be
the world's best carpenter. Everything you make will
be beautiful." He turned back to his work.

"Ah, then," asked Jesus, "do you think I will someday
make a beautiful yoke—one that will be easy for
the oxen to wear? One that will not hurt them?"

Joseph smiled as he answered, "Jesus, you will make
many yokes when you are a carpenter, and every one you
make will be easy to bear. I think that you will work
with such care that everything you make will be beautiful."

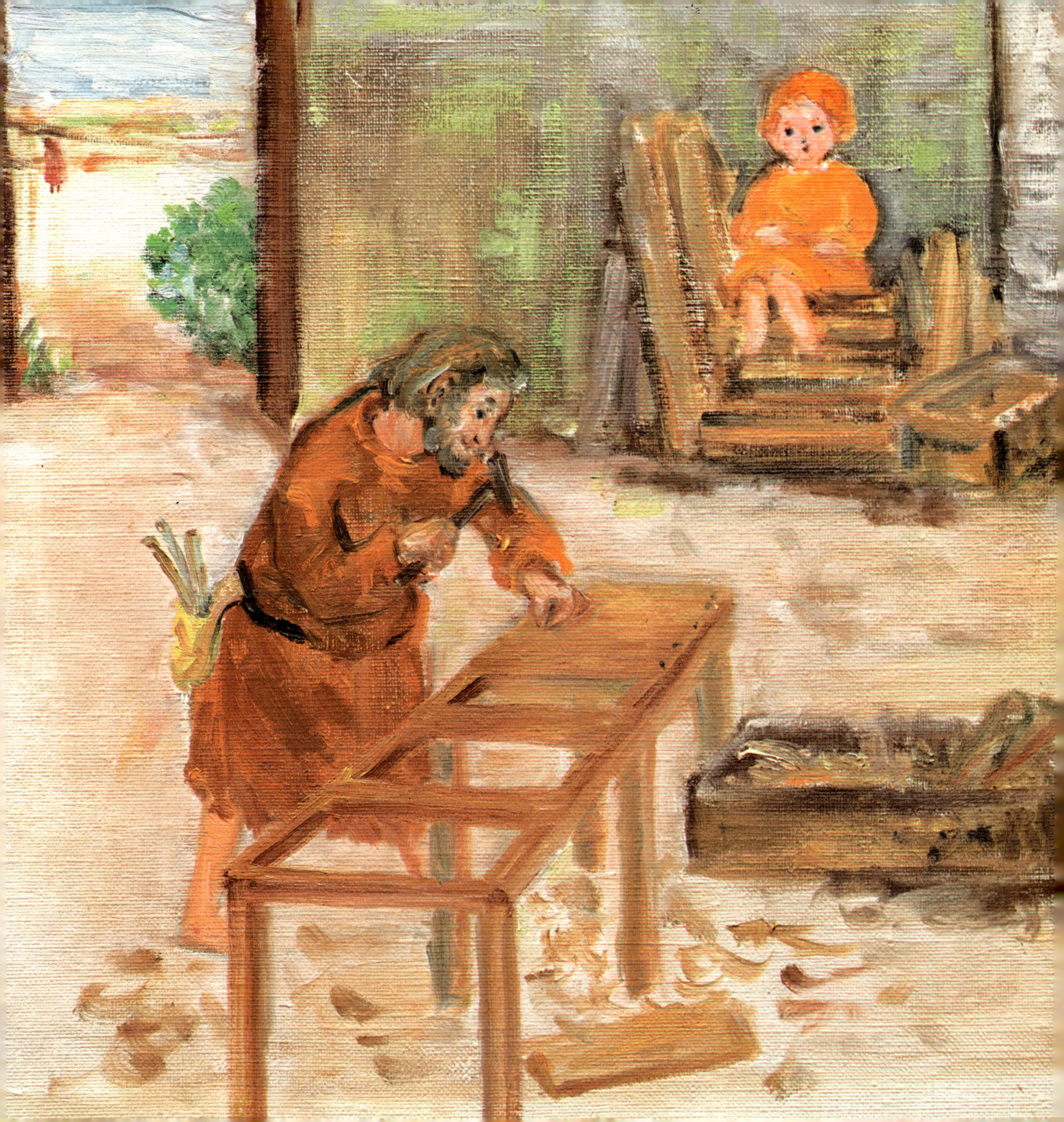

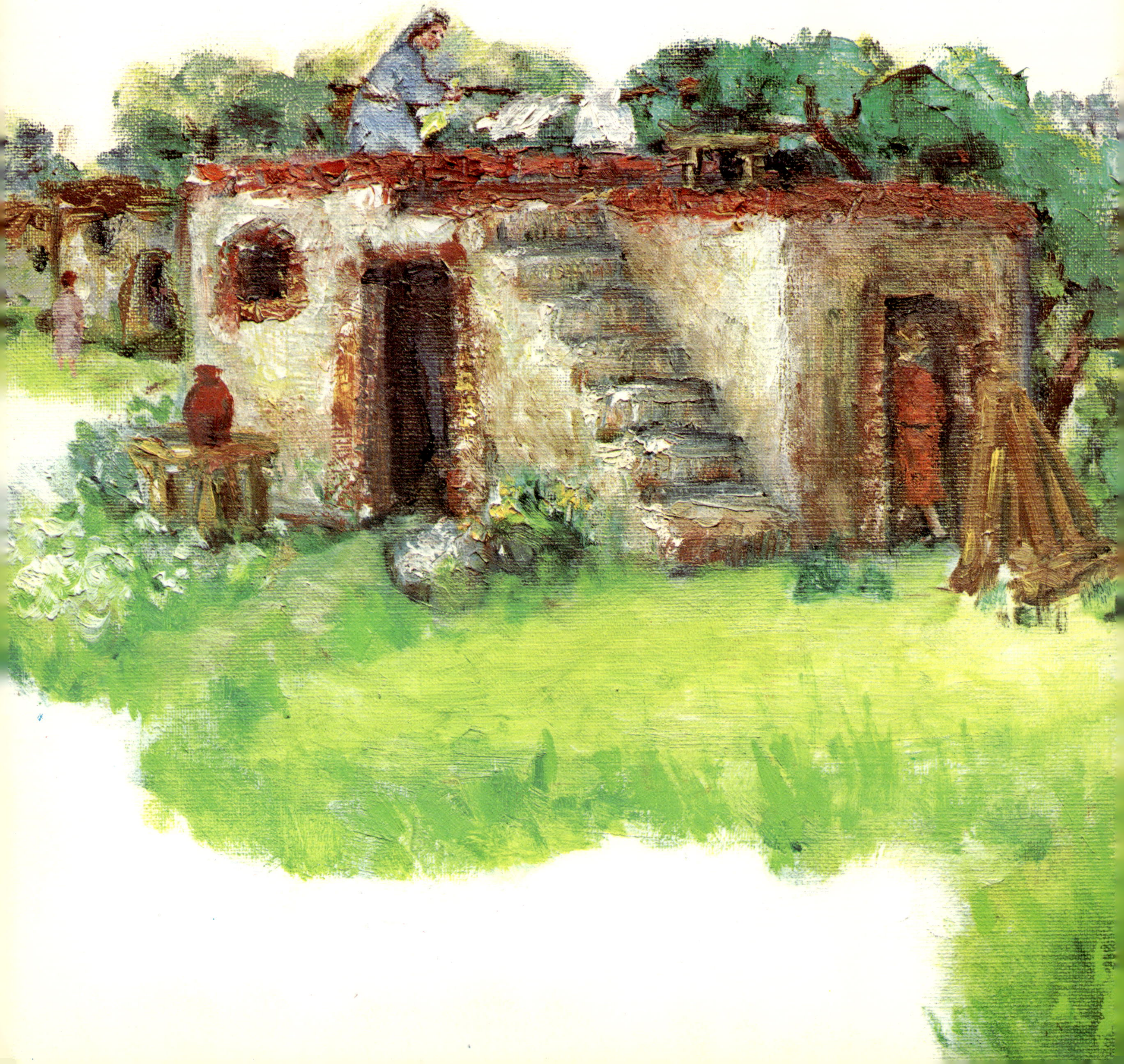

"Look, Mother," called Jesus. "I have picked some juicy berries! Let's have a party! We can have berries and honey and goat's milk. We can have our party under the shade of our big tree. Please, Mother, may we? Shall I call Father?"

"All right, Jesus," answered Mary. "But before you call Father, let's get everything ready. Let's make it a surprise for him!"

As they sat together enjoying the party Jesus
had planned, Mary and Joseph listened to him tell
about his day.

"I love the springtime," Jesus said happily.
"The hills are covered with flowers.
The bees were so happy there. They buzzed and
made beautiful music. They didn't seem to care
if I picked berries for us.

"I was not afraid of them at all.
And they were not afraid of me, either.
It was fun!"

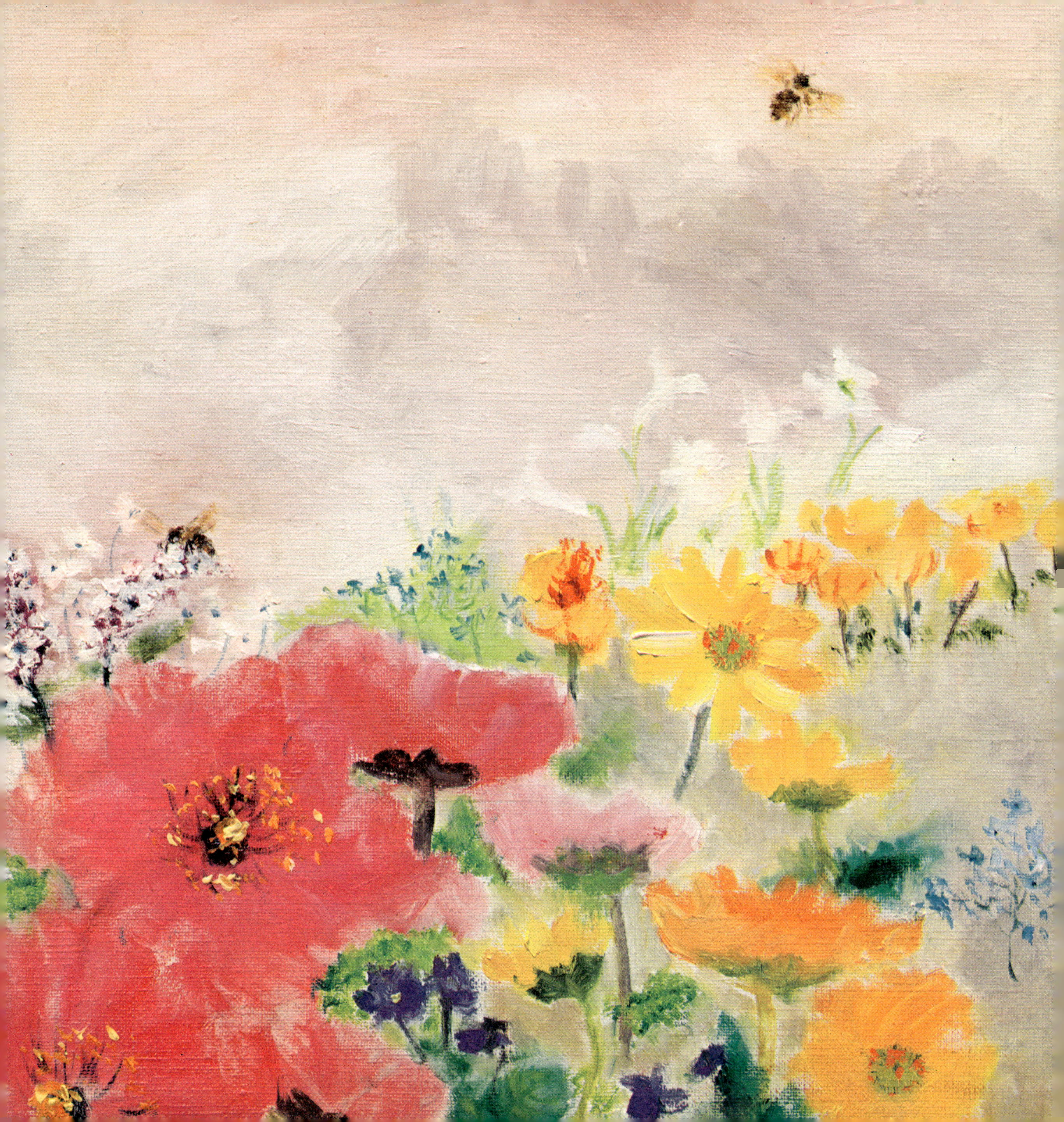

"Hurry, Mother," said Jesus. "I can see our friends at the well! While you get water and talk with the other mothers, I can play in the grass with my friends. And then, oh, Mother, then will you tell us a story?"

Mary laughed at Jesus' excitement. "Yes, Jesus," she said. "Today there will be time for a story."

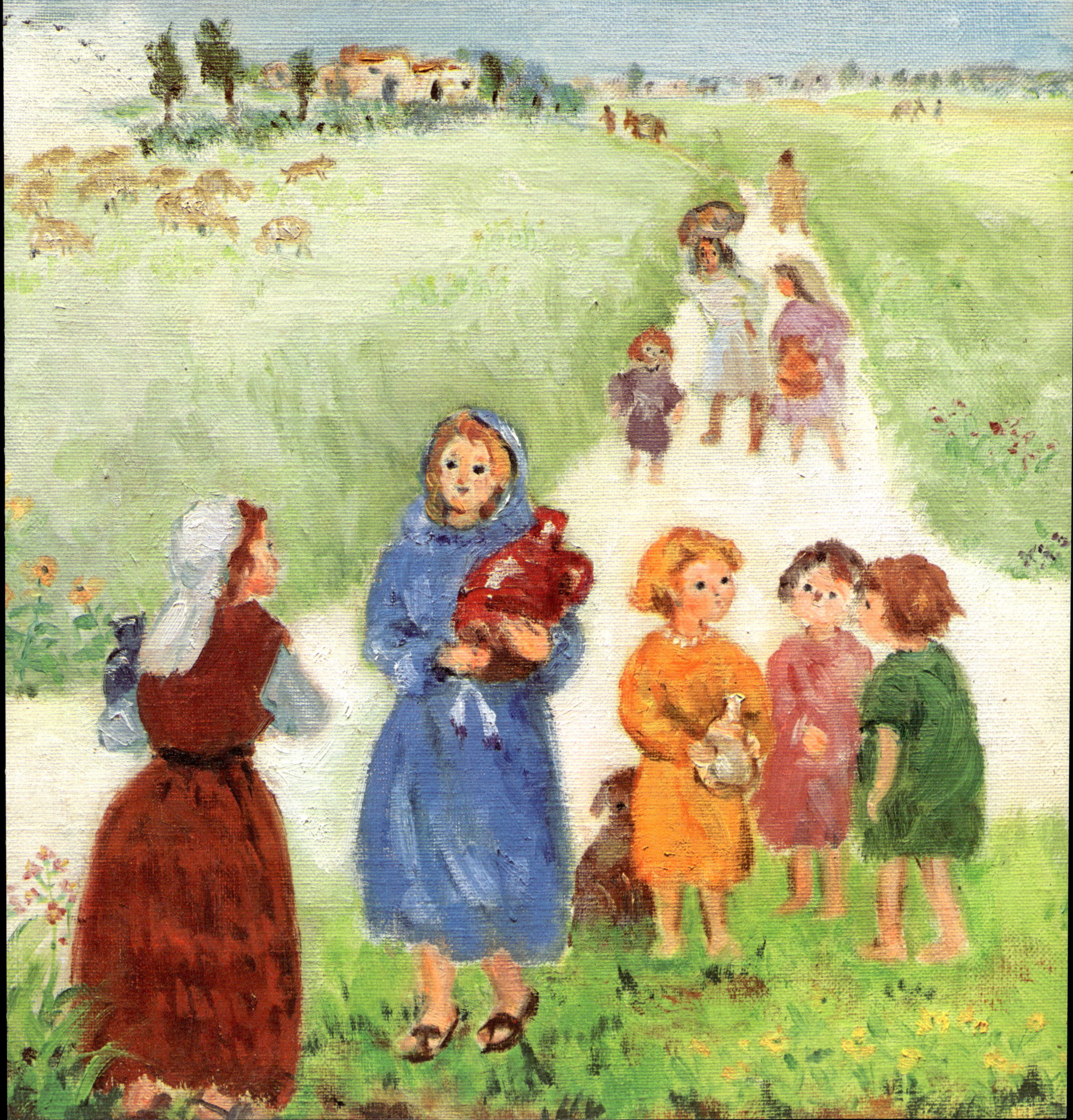

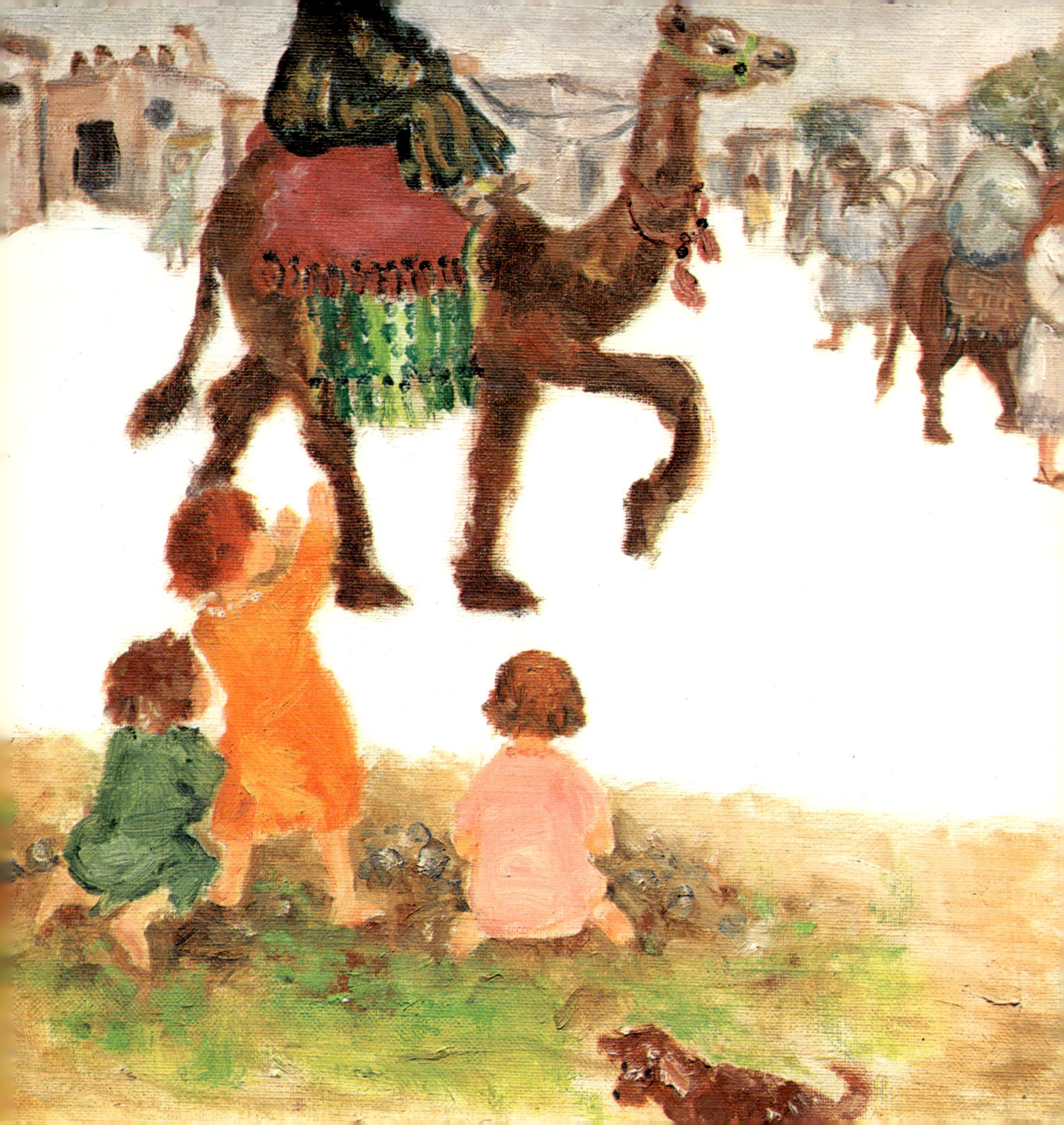

It was market day in Nazareth. Jesus and his friends watched and watched. It seemed that people had come from all over the world. Some of them looked so tired.

Clump-clump! Clump-clump! A camel passed by them.

"Oh, what a great camel you are!" said Jesus. "When I get big, I will ride on a camel. I hope he is as beautiful a camel as you are!"

Clump-clump! Clump-clump! Soon the camel was out of sight.

But there were so many other things to watch!

"Everyone must work hard today," thought Jesus as he watched the sheep. "The seeds must be planted. They seem to die in the ground, but Mother says they don't really die. She says that soon they will send up green shoots. Then they will grow straight and tall. They will make beautiful fields. They will give us good food."

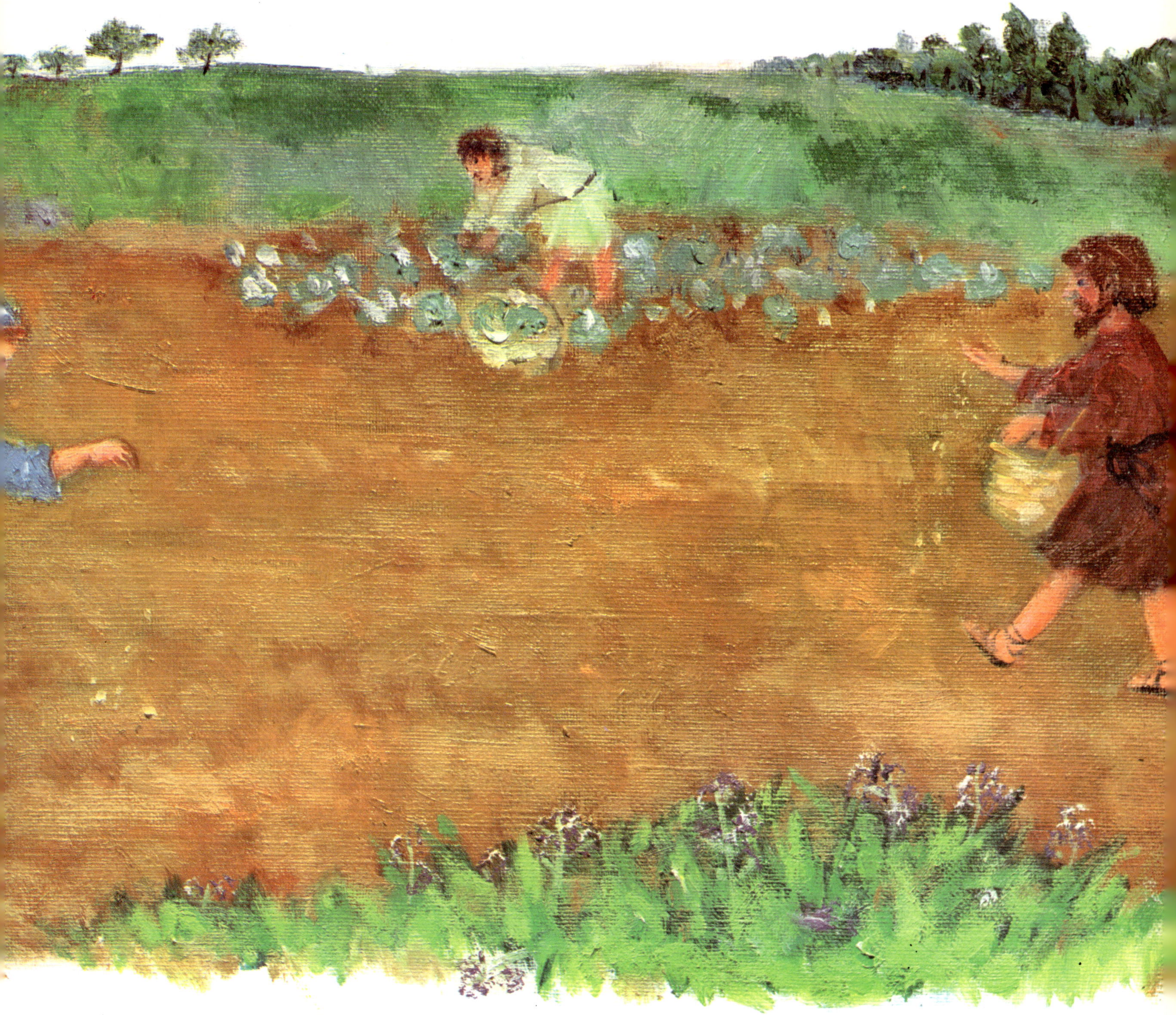

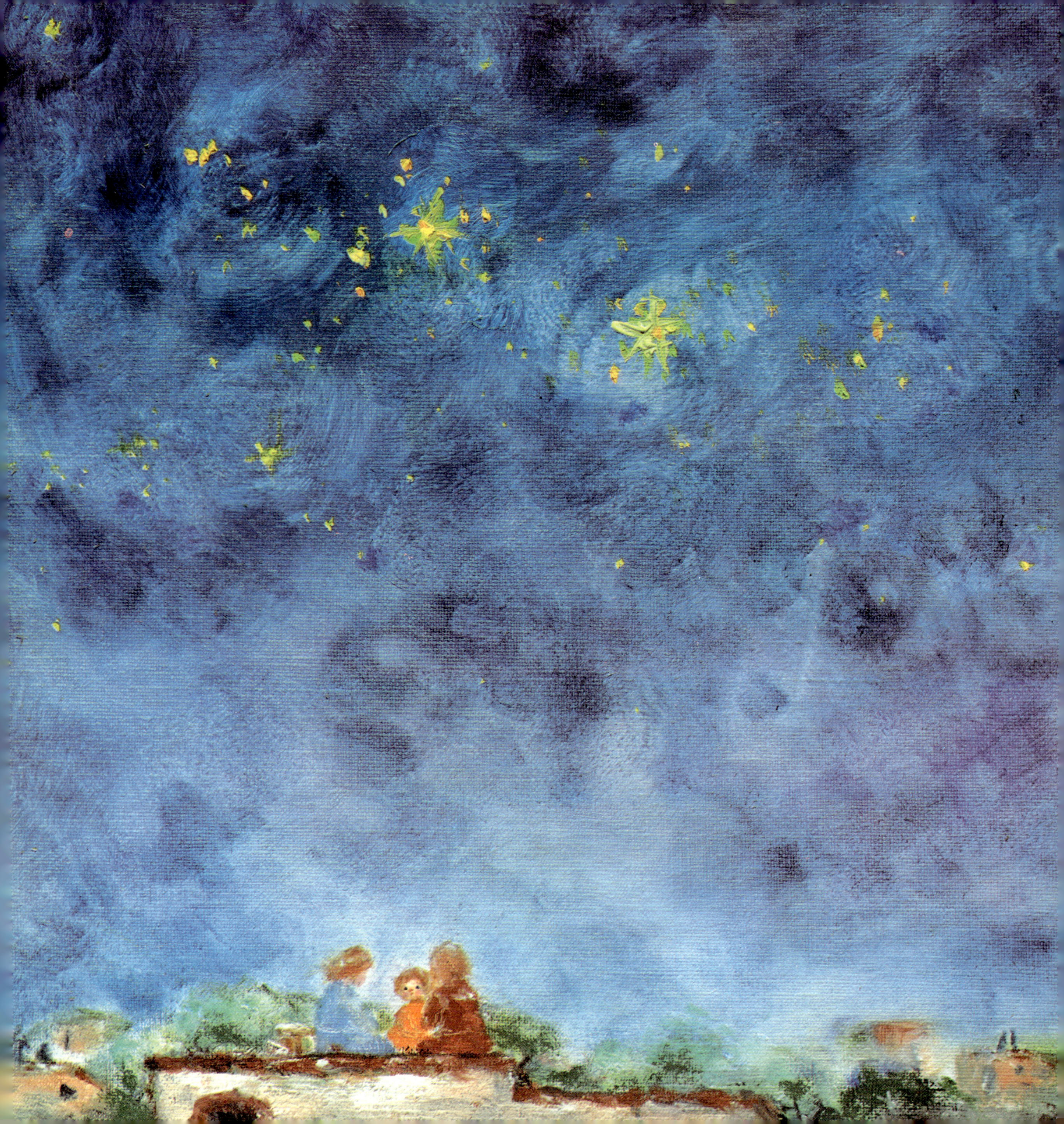

At night under the stars, Jesus and Mary and Joseph sat
and talked about the things that had happened that day.
They talked to each other. Then they talked to God
in prayer.

This was a special night. Tomorrow Jesus would start
to go to school. Jesus and Mary and Joseph were all
quiet as they listened to the sounds of the night.

"The sounds of the night are so different from the
sounds of the day," thought Jesus. "I wonder what
school will be like? But I must not let my mother and
father know I am afraid."

Jesus bowed his head.
"Please, dear Father in Heaven," he prayed,
"even though we must be away from each other
part of the time, help us always to know that
we are close to you. Amen."

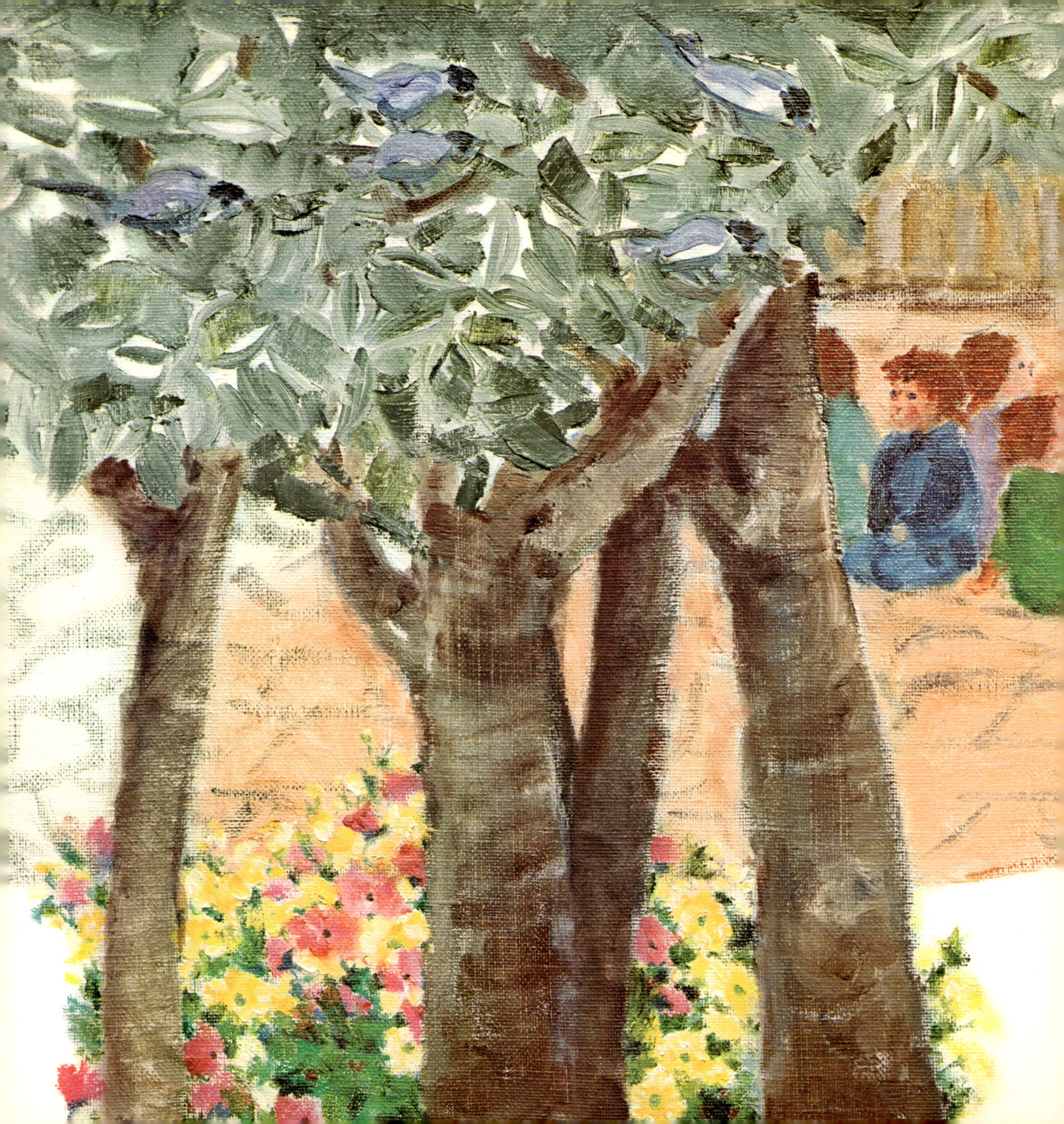

Jesus found that he liked school. There were many new things to think about.

"Will you tell us new things every day, Teacher?" he asked. "Will you tell us more about our Father in Heaven? Will you———"

His teacher laughed. "Yes, Jesus," he said. "We will learn many things together."

"How was school today?" asked Mary as they all sat together under the stars.

"It was fun! We learned lots of things, but I don't think I remember them all yet. My teacher said that he knew you. He said you were very good teachers. And he asked me what I wanted to be when I grew up."

"And what did you answer, Jesus?" asked Joseph.

"I told him that I might be a carpenter like you are. I told him that I would make everything beautiful, because my father told me so!"

AS JESUS GREW

Mildred Schell
Takeshi Sakuma

1 When Jesus was a boy in Nazareth,
  Each single day brought him new things to do;
  He learned that growing up is fun to do—
  And so-o can you.

2 No matter where you live in all this world,
  Your every day may bring surprises, too;
  And you will find that you are growing up
  As Je-e-sus grew.

(NOTE: excess letters in last line to indicate two notes to one syllable.)